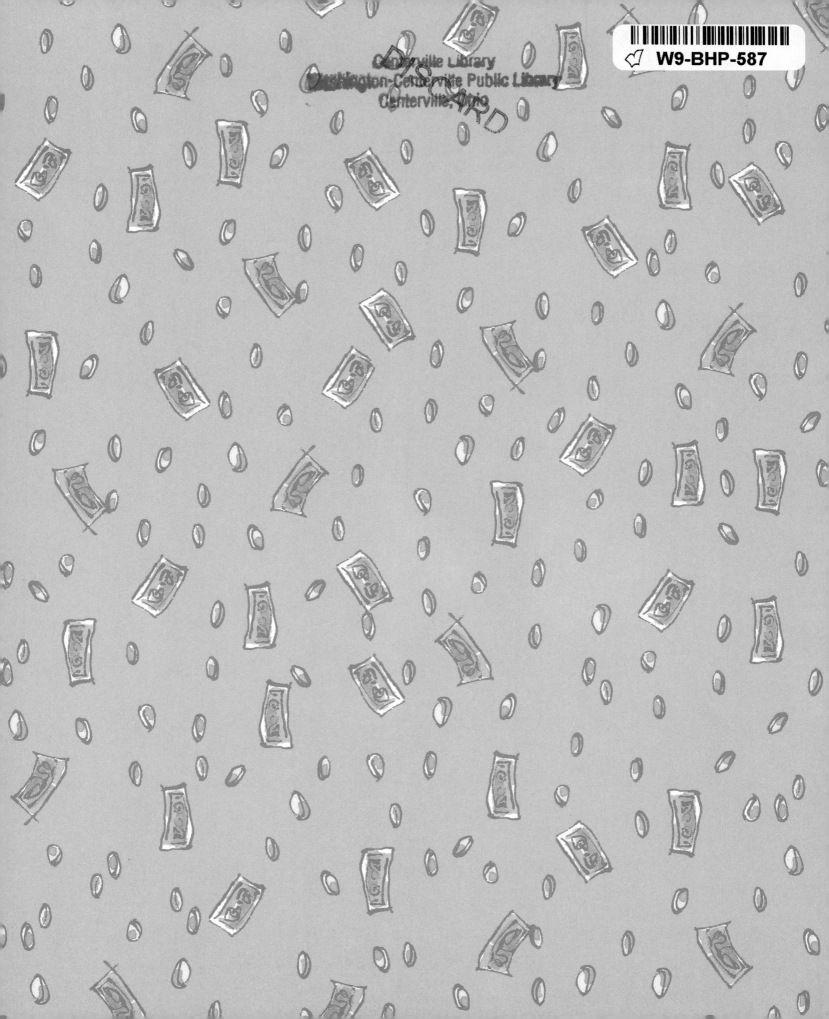

Centerville Library
Washington-Centerville Public Library
Centerville, Ohio

DISCARD

W9-BHP-587

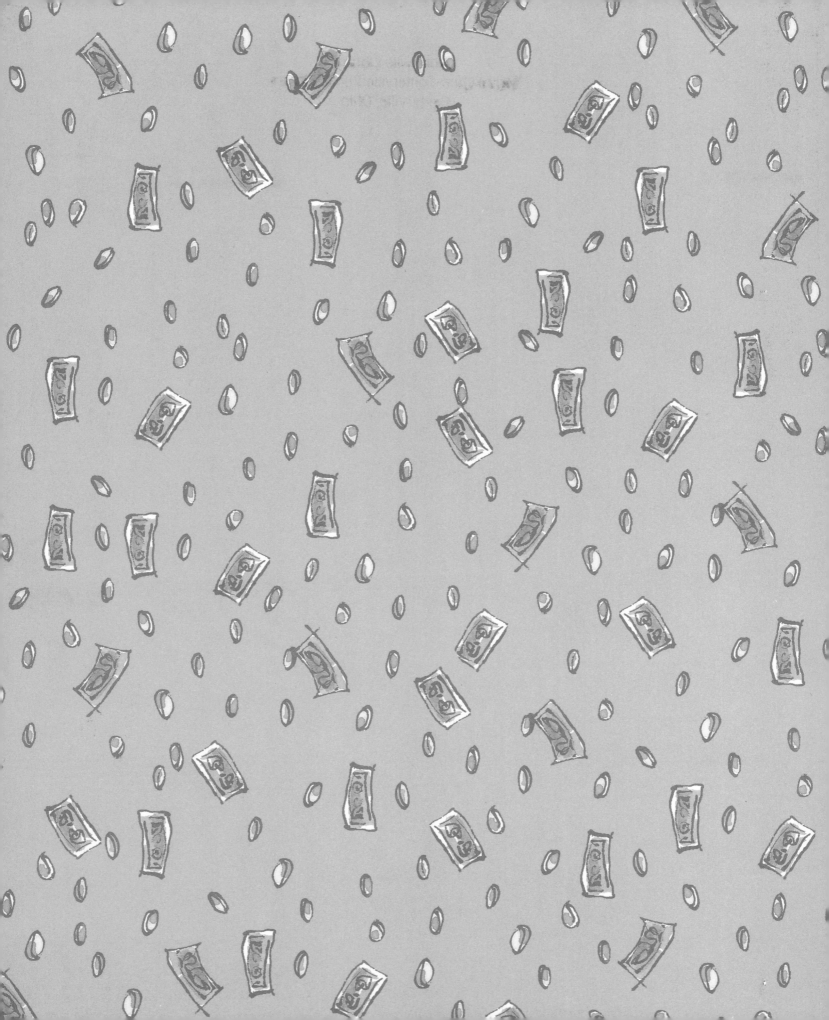

Common Cents

The Money in Your Pocket

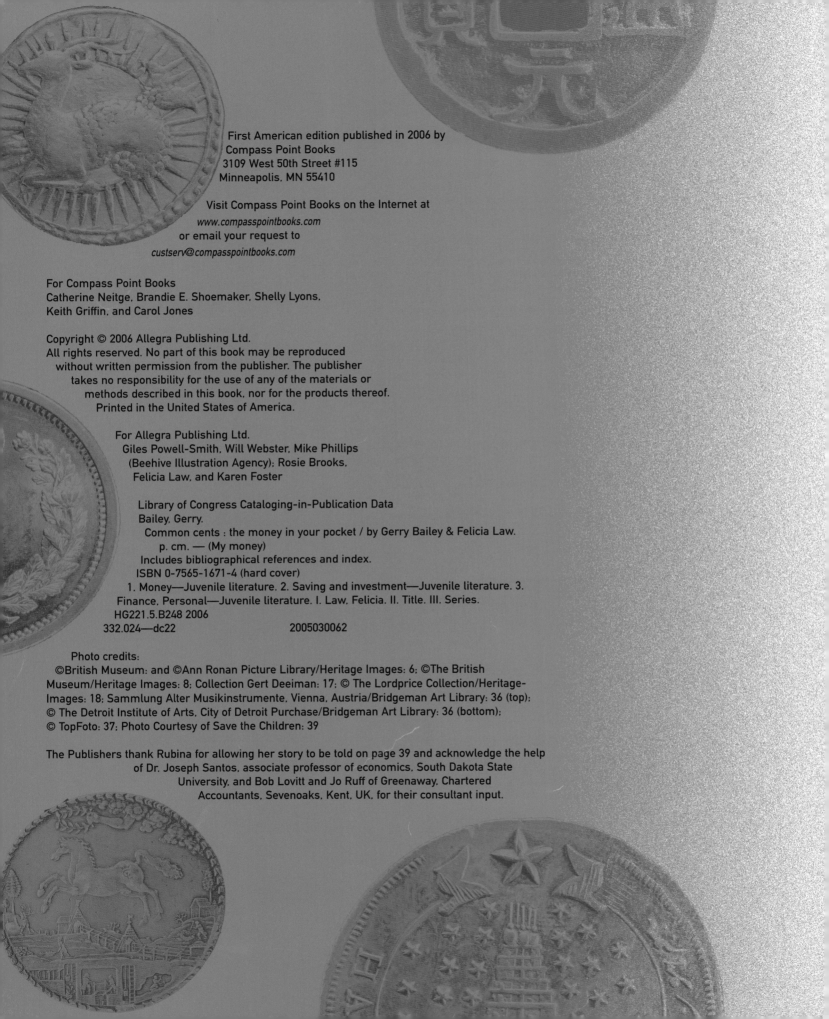

First American edition published in 2006 by
Compass Point Books
3109 West 50th Street #115
Minneapolis, MN 55410

Visit Compass Point Books on the Internet at
www.compasspointbooks.com
or email your request to
custserv@compasspointbooks.com

For Compass Point Books
Catherine Neitge, Brandie E. Shoemaker, Shelly Lyons,
Keith Griffin, and Carol Jones

Copyright © 2006 Allegra Publishing Ltd.
All rights reserved. No part of this book may be reproduced
without written permission from the publisher. The publisher
takes no responsibility for the use of any of the materials or
methods described in this book, nor for the products thereof.
Printed in the United States of America.

For Allegra Publishing Ltd.
Giles Powell-Smith, Will Webster, Mike Phillips
(Beehive Illustration Agency): Rosie Brooks,
Felicia Law, and Karen Foster

Library of Congress Cataloging-in-Publication Data
Bailey, Gerry.
  Common cents : the money in your pocket / by Gerry Bailey & Felicia Law.
    p. cm. — (My money)
  Includes bibliographical references and index.
  ISBN 0-7565-1671-4 (hard cover)
  1. Money—Juvenile literature. 2. Saving and investment—Juvenile literature. 3.
Finance, Personal—Juvenile literature. I. Law, Felicia. II. Title. III. Series.
  HG221.5.B248 2006
  332.024—dc22   2005030062

Photo credits:
©British Museum: and ©Ann Ronan Picture Library/Heritage Images: 6; ©The British
Museum/Heritage Images: 8; Collection Gert Deeiman: 17; © The Lordprice Collection/Heritage-
Images: 18; Sammlung Alter Musikinstrumente, Vienna, Austria/Bridgeman Art Library: 36 (top);
© The Detroit Institute of Arts, City of Detroit Purchase/Bridgeman Art Library: 36 (bottom);
© TopFoto: 37; Photo Courtesy of Save the Children: 39

The Publishers thank Rubina for allowing her story to be told on page 39 and acknowledge the help
of Dr. Joseph Santos, associate professor of economics, South Dakota State
University, and Bob Lovitt and Jo Ruff of Greenaway, Chartered
Accountants, Sevenoaks, Kent, UK, for their consultant input.

Common Cents

Gerry Bailey & Felicia Law

You're young, you're bright, and you've got
money! Where did the money in your pocket
come from, and just how are you
going to make it work for you?

COMPASS POINT BOOKS MINNEAPOLIS, MINNESOTA

Money is a must! It's something you can take control of, have fun with, grow, spend, save, and help people with. And it's never too early to start!

Table of Contents

What is money?

The obvious answer to this question is that money is the stuff jingling in your pocket or purse, as well as the dollar bills that seem to vanish as quickly as you get them. But if the coins and paper bills were from another country and couldn't buy you as much as a bus ticket at home, would you still call them money? And what about checks? Of course, you'd rather have the coins and bills anytime, but pieces of paper like checks that promise "to act as money" are by far the most popular form of money in the world today. Then there's credit cards and gold—that's money, isn't it? There's even a form of money that you can't even see or touch—electronic money. Is all this really money?

Chinese tool-shaped coin

Cowrie shells

5,000 years of money!

As we find out just what is and what isn't seen as money today, we'll discover that all sorts of crazy forms of money have cropped up in the past—amber, beads, cowrie shells, drums, eggs, and feathers, to name just a few. Money has been around in one form or another for 5,000 years! The fact is that money wasn't just invented in one place. It developed in all kinds of ways and in many different parts of the world. But no matter what object was used as money, it always had four attributes:

Feather coil used by the Pacific islanders of Santa Cruz

- Everyone agreed to use it.
- Everyone agreed that it could be used in different ways to pay for goods, to reward people, to bribe them, and so on.
- Everyone agreed that it had a value that wouldn't change from day to day.
- Everyone agreed to respect what it stood for.

Chinese coin sword. Brass coins are attached to a rod using lucky string.

And so ...

It doesn't take much to see that money is still changing its shape and form, even if it's not as dramatic as cowrie shell to check! Also, money isn't being used in the same way everywhere. This is mainly because money isn't just about currency—coins and bills—or even credit cards. It's about banks, savings and loans, mortgage companies that lend money for house purchases, employment agencies, and lots more. Money holds us all together—working, spending, saving, and traveling. In fact, money is the link between you and thousands of other people—absolute strangers—all of whom affect your life!

Big changes ahead!

In your own lifetime, you might just see the end of those jingling coins and paper bills. Technology is now learning to cope with the huge money transactions that speed around our planet on a minute by minute basis. There are likely to be more changes to the look and feel of money in the next 10 years than in the past 5,000!

Money is a must!

Do you have money? Do you have money jingling in your pocket today? A wallet full of coins and bills? A savings or bank account of your own? Or a piggy bank where you pop all those spare coins?

If you have any of these, you have money! And it's likely that you'll have more and more money as the months and years go by. Money is like water—it flows freely—in and out of everyone's pockets, and in every country of the world. It will definitely flow in and out of your pocket your entire life, but will it flow out faster than it flows in? That's the problem everyone has to deal with!

If it flows in, you're earning or receiving. You may have to work for the money, or you may be given it as a gift or a grant.

If it flows out, you're spending. You're buying things and paying for them. If it flows in faster than it flows out, you'll be rich. If it doesn't, you'll have problems. Lots of them! Nobody can decide these things for you— it's all up to you.

The more you know about money, the better you'll be able to decide for yourself. And the more you understand, the more control over your money you'll have.

Money's fun, too! Earning it is fun, and spending it is definitely fun! But you can do better that this. You can "grow" money, or invest it. Now that's a real challenge! And you can spend it in special ways. You can spend it so that you earn on it at the same time. That's an even bigger challenge! Or you can share it. You can share it with people who will be helped in a really big way. Imagine being able to help someone like that!

Money is a must. It's something you can't escape from, but this doesn't have to be a bad thing. Just the opposite—it's something you can take control of, have fun with, grow, spend, and help people with.

And it's never too early to start!

Look! No cash!

The Inca were an ancient Indian people that lived in the Andes Mountains of South America.

The Inca of Peru managed very nicely without money. Their money, as such, existed only in the form of work. Each person paid taxes by working on the roads, fields, irrigation canals, temples, and fortresses. In return, Inca rulers paid their laborers in clothing and food.

Silver and gold were abundant, but only used for display.

Money's been around for 5,000 years! Watch this space for more amazing money facts!

Artemis

Artemis, the shepherd, stopped dead in his tracks. There, in the tailor's window, was the outfit he wanted. It was super-cool, and the label said it all— Must have!

Must have!

"The outfit in the window ... What can I swap you for it?" Artemis asked the tailor.

"What are you offering?" said the tailor. "It depends on what you've got."

"I've got the usual shepherd gear," said Artemis. "Loads of sheep, hardly used, very woolly."

"Ancient! Nobody wants that woolly stuff. And all that baa-ing and bleating would drive me crazy."

"Well, what else will you take?" asked Artemis, not taking his eyes off the outfit in the window.

"Have you got any food? I can always use something to eat."

"Cheese?" said Artemis. "Sheep's cheese. I've got more than I want."

"Terrible!" said the tailor. "That cheese stuff stinks."

"Well I must have something you want," stormed Artemis in desperation. "What do you take from other customers?"

"Got any cash?" asked the tailor. "You know, those round, metal discs with people's heads on? Coins, they call them. You can trade them as swaps for most things."

That settled it! Artemis had to get some coins. And as long as both he and the tailor agreed what the coins were worth and were happy to exchange, they were in business.

So a few coins saved the day. Artemis got what he wanted, and the tailor got something useful in exchange.

Barter

Swapping, or bartering, is a good way for two people to get the things they want from each other. You probably do this all the time. You swap a card in your collection for one you haven't got, a lipstick you don't use for a color you will, a "bad buy" skirt for a friend's coat she can't get into.

But barter is restricting. You can only trade or swap using things you actually have, and you may not have the very thing the person you're swapping with wants! Not everyone who wants what you have has what you want! Confusing, isn't it?

Given all this, it's surprising that barter lasted as long as it did and in so many societies. You can see that it's a clumsy way to buy what you want. And you can understand why coins became so popular and widely used for trading once they were invented.

Trading with coins

Early money, made out of metal, was usually molded into the shape of a small round disk. We call it a coin. The invention of coins made it easy to put a value on anything: clothes, food, housing, even sheep. And coins have other advantages.

- Coins are made of something that's rare and not too easy to get. This gives coins value from the start.
- Coins are difficult to counterfeit, or copy, especially if they are stamped with a design.
- Coins are easy to carry around. Well, easier than sheep anyway!
- Different sizes of coins made from different materials can have different values—a gold coin can be worth five times more than a silver one.

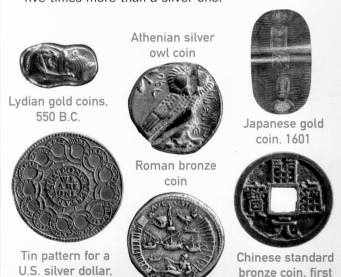

Lydian gold coins, 550 B.C.

Athenian silver owl coin

Japanese gold coin, 1601

Roman bronze coin

Tin pattern for a U.S. silver dollar, 1776

Chinese standard bronze coin, first issued A.D. 621

The functions of money

So, since money is different things to different people, let's look at what money **DOES** rather than what it **IS**.

• Money is a unit of account

This simply means that money provides us with a way of adding up our wealth or giving something a price or value.

• Money offers a standard for delayed payments

If you don't settle a payment at once, you can agree to pay later. The amount you owe can be agreed to in a form that both you and the lender accept—in money.

• Money is a common measure of value

This means you can put a value on a coin that everyone accepts. When coins were made out of precious metals, this solved the problem easily. Coins were, quite literally, worth whatever they weighed in silver or gold.

But today, coins cost far less to produce than the value marked on them. It doesn't necessarily cost 1 cent to mine, smelt, forge, and stamp a 1 cent coin. What is important is that everyone who uses a 1 cent coin accepts that they can use it to buy things that cost 1 cent. In other words, the value of money is what it will buy.

• Money lets you store value

You don't want to spend all your wealth at once. You might like to put some away for a rainy day. Whether your wealth is measured in cows or cheese, it can still be regarded as money. But your cows might get sick, and their value would decrease. If your money were measured in cheese, it could have an even shorter life! Money in coin or note form doesn't get sick or get moldy! It's a good way to store your wealth so it holds its value.

• Money is a medium of exchange

You can seal a bargain in feathers, eggs, shells—or coins—as long as both parties agree.

Coins take over

Coins were in use long before they replaced barter. Although they weren't used in trade, they were used to keep the enemy quiet. The verb "to pay" comes from the Latin word *pacare*, which originally meant to pacify, or make peace with. If a tribe wanted to make peace with another, it had to pay for that peace by using a unit of value acceptable to both sides. Early coins were used to do this.

Another widespread custom that needed coins was payment for a bride. This compensated the head of the family for the loss of a daughter's help in the home.

So coins, which were originally accepted for all these different uses, also began to be used for general trading—and in time they replaced barter altogether.

Spend, save, share

A coin is just a piece of metal until you use it to make something happen. You can use it in just three different ways: You either spend it, save it, or give it away. Each of these will bring different results.

Spending

We all love spending money. It gives us the things we want, it makes us feel good—and it's not that difficult! There's no shortage of things to spend your money on. But just in case you've run out of ideas, you're bombarded with ads on the street, in magazines, on TV—and when you've actually bought something—even on your shopping bags.

But spending money brings a certain responsibility. You can only spend the money you have. If you're careful with your spending, everything's fine. If you're reckless, you can end up in trouble. When grown-ups lecture you about understanding the value of money, it's really this that they're talking about—knowing how to spend wisely.

Spending puts your money into circulation. You pass money across a counter for goods. The store clerk passes it to the bank, which passes it to people who buy things—and so on and so on.

Saving

For many people, saving isn't nearly as easy as spending. Some even talk about saving as if it's the opposite of spending. Perhaps it feels that way—instead of losing $10 out of your pocket, you have gained $10 by holding on to it. But it's not so simple.

Does saving to you mean stashing your cash in your mattress? Or do you pop a portion of your money in a piggy bank on a regular basis? Then at least the stash will grow, even if slowly.

However, there are ways of saving, which, just like spending, involve putting your money into circulation. When you put your money into a savings account at the bank, you are trusting someone else to make it grow. The bank invests it in business deals and it tries to earn a profit—a good one. And some of that profit is given back to you.

Sharing

Sharing is something you usually do because you want to, not because you have to. Handouts to friends are probably done knowing your friends will return the favor sometime. But it feels good to actually help someone who desperately needs it. There are plenty of people in this situation.

Dropping a few coins into a charity box each week means that someone somewhere will be helped by YOU. And you could get directly involved and actually see how your contribution is helping. We hear news every day of terrible poverty and hunger in countries all around the world. You can shrug this off as being someone else's problem—it's all too far away. And anyway, why can't their governments help them? But when a few people have a lot of money and most people are begging for food, things certainly seem unbalanced.

It IS possible to change things. We can each do a little, knowing that this will add up to a lot in the end.

Cost of living

What we do with our money is all about choice. Or is it? Unfortunately, we need money to stay alive, and here we don't have many choices. Spending some of our money on shelter and food is a necessity. In fact, most people find that most of their money is spent on necessities and that only a small amount is left for saving and sharing.

So figuring out how much these necessities will cost is essential. Prices can go up and down, and people's earnings can go up and down, so how do they do it?

One way people keep tabs on what money can buy at any time is by using a measure called the cost of living. This means just what it says—how much it costs us to live. But how and what we spend has changed over the years. Just look at a family budget from the past:

Fred and Myrtle—1913

Fred earns $10 a week as a clerk. Myrtle is a housewife. This is how they spend their money:

60% on food = $6
12% on clothing = $1.20
16% on rent = $1.60
8% on fuel/electricity = 80¢
4% on everything else = 40¢

They spent most of their money on food. They had very little left over for treats or luxuries. In fact, it took 96% of their earnings just to make ends meet.

John and Elizabeth—2006

John is a computer programmer. Elizabeth is a teacher. Together they earn $1,035 a week. They spend the following:

25% on mortgage = $259
18% on food = $186
4% on fuel/electricity = $41
4% on gas/necessary travel = $41
20% on cars = $207
29% on everything else = $300

Compare the two budgets and look how things have changed—not just the amount that families earn, but what they spend their money on.

The honey guide's revenge

An old Zulu tale from South Africa tells about sharing.

Once there was a greedy young man named Gingile who never shared anything with anybody. He kept his corn and his meat to himself.

While out hunting one day, Gingile heard the chitik-chitik honey call of Ngede, the honey guide. His mouth watered at the thought of sweet honey.

When the little bird saw that Gingile was interested, he began moving through the branches toward the honey nest. Gingile quickly made a fire and soon had a smoking branch. He scurried up the tree, found the nest, and poked it in.

With a furious buzzing the bees flew out of the nest, and Gingile was able to reach in his hand and bring out luscious pieces of honeycomb.

Once Gingile was back on the ground, Ngede waited patiently for his share, but Gingile said, "I've done all the work, so why should you have any?" And off he went, leaving behind a furious and hungry honey guide.

"How dare he break the custom?" thought Ngede. "Honey guides always get their share!" Ngede had to wait several moons to get his revenge.

One day, Gingile heard the sound of the honey guide again and followed the little bird to a great umbrella tree. Gingile prepared his smoking branch and climbed the tree as before. But this time there were no buzzing bees. Instead he came face to face with a resting leopard. The leopard woke up and swiped out with a paw, raking Gingile's forehead.

Gingile bore the marks for the rest of his life. Never again would he cheat a honey guide.

Pocket money

The older you are, the more likely you are to want money of your own. Most teenagers depend primarily on their parents for support. Your parents probably don't charge you to live and eat in the family home, and they may buy some of your school supplies, but most prefer to give you an allowance and let you look after your own personal expenses. It's never too early to learn how to handle money—and how to save.

What about making your bed ...

But increasingly as you get older, there's pressure from all kinds of companies that want you to buy their stuff—and from some of your friends who've already got it! Even if you take a sensible view of all this, there comes a time when little gifts from fond aunts and handouts from parents just aren't enough. It's time to establish a proper arrangement at home. Your parents may give you a weekly allowance from the family money, in return for you taking responsibility for certain chores around the house.

... or washing the dishes ...

Oh, those chores!

So, with pocket money comes responsibility. If pocket money has strings attached, which require you to carry out certain chores, it's worth making a contract with your parents that details EXACTLY what they expect of you. Once you've agreed what they pay for and what they don't, they'll expect you to stick to this.

Chores may involve simply helping around the kitchen or keeping your own room clean—which you should be doing anyway! They may involve taking care of pets or working in the garden. They'll certainly help your parents out and involve you in taking on some of the workload of the household. No problem! You're getting paid for it!

A regular income

Pocket money is your first step to receiving a regular income. It can be relied on to come in each week, more or less on time, and in full. You can "bank on it," as they say, which also means you can be planning how you're going to spend it long before it arrives.

You may like to receive a weekly or monthly allowance, depending on how the family budget is arranged. It will also depend on how far you can trust yourself to stick to a budget. It's no good taking a monthly amount if you can't trust yourself not to blow it all in the first week!

And one more thing: How much pocket money you get depends on how much money your parents have available to give you, or how much they think you should have. Accept pocket money as you would accept a gift. After all, that's what it really is. Even if it's a small amount, it's worth showing that you're grateful.

... or taking the dog for a walk.

Are you getting an allowance?

There are different opinions about the value of giving allowances or pocket money to young people, and you may find your parents need a little persuasion.

The parent perspective

You may have parents who already know all of this—they believe it's important for you to start handling your own money at a young age. They may be giving you a regular allowance or have regular expectations of you—the kind of contract discussed before. Perhaps they just hand out cash whenever you ask for it—or more likely, whenever you pressure them into giving it you! This is treating you like a child. You want to move on!

They do have a point. They may both be working in jobs themselves—and since you enjoy the benefits of their earnings, surely helping make life easier for everyone is the least that can be asked of you. The trouble is that when you don't quite live up to expectations—you forget to make your bed, turn off the lights downstairs, or put the cat out— they can use this point against you. Then you get upset, and arguments develop. How much simpler when everyone knows what's expected of them! You do the chores. They pay you pocket money.

As for giving you wads of cash just because you ask for it, or because they like doing it—they're doing you no favors. It's unlikely you'll grow up in a world where wads of cash continue to come your way free of effort and responsibilities. So why train you to have unreal expectations or encourage you to adopt bad habits? Surely that's not their intention!

Thanks, Dad. It's a deal!

On the other hand, there are parents who think that helping with the household chores should be part of your involvement anyway, and aren't happy about having to pay you for this.

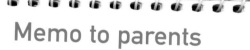

Memo to parents

Using pocket money
- Having pocket money is good for your child.
- It encourages a sense of independence.
- It helps kids understand the value of money.
- It teaches them to make decisions on whether to spend it all right away, or save for a few weeks so they can buy something special.

Ages and stages
Increase pocket money by a fixed amount on each birthday. If your child is old enough to help out with household chores, arrange increases to pocket money in exchange for more involvement.

Stick to the rules
Your children have a strong sense of what's fair. So don't give in and buy extras for one child who's already spent all of her money, when another child has had to save for his treats.

The importance of money

Money is important in our lives:

- We think about it and talk about it.
- We love having it and couldn't buy much without it.
- We need it for necessities like food and shelter.
- We enjoy it for the fun things it buys.

Enough!

The amount of money we need varies from person to person—but everybody needs some! In fact, life would come to an abrupt halt without it. Researchers report that many people believe they have enough money. And lots of people think money isn't everything.

Having said that, young people like you are responsible for spending billions around the globe each year. Money is going to play a huge part in your life, so it's best you know as much as possible about it.

Are you a saver or a spender?

It's amazing how some people can save money easily. It seems to come naturally to them. People can be as different about the way they handle money as they are in the way they look or the things they're interested in. If you're not a natural saver, it can be frustrating to be with people who are. They always seem to have cash available when you're broke. Not fun! Equally, if you're happy to see your money fly straight out of your hands into your wardrobe or your video games—even into your stomach—it's unlikely you'll change your ways just because everyone tells you that you should! But you might like to weigh the pros and cons of saving and spending.

The small saver

- You spend, but you weigh what you need against what you want.
- Maybe you do without the occasional luxury so you can save a bit.
- The money you save begins to add up.
- And the more you have, the better you feel about it.
- You can still buy a few things when you want to.
- You can deal with emergencies, like a flat bike tire.
- You can buy things that you couldn't afford with just a week's, or a month's, pocket money.
- You're learning life skills.

The big spender

- You spend and spend, and blow all of your money.
- You feel good, you look good, you've got lots of stuff.
- You look big and successful to your friends.
- You've got power in your pocket —for the moment.
- And when it's all gone, you come down with a bump.
- You never have anything saved for emergencies.
- You never have enough for the one thing you've always wanted but just can't afford.
- You overdo your spending and sometimes have to borrow.

Spending power

How much pocket money you receive and what you do with it is likely to vary from country to country. But almost every country can agree on two things—the number of young people in the population is growing, and the money they are spending is increasing fast. Manufacturers are rushing to grab a share of this market, producing products and advertising them with the young person in mind. It's clear that they're succeeding!

Unbelievably, how teenagers decide to spend that money can close a movie, sink a retail chain, bury a product, send a rock star to oblivion, or alter the eating choices of a nation. The role of young people in the economies of the world is growing. Increasingly, they will have more and more to say about the shape of future markets.

Let's look at what happens in the United States:

- In five years, spending by American teenagers jumped from $122 billion a year to $170 billion. (Remember, 1 billion is 1,000 million.)
- Of this spending in 2002, $125 million was teenagers' own money, with the rest coming from parents.
- Between now and the year 2010, the number of young consumers is expected to grow from 31 million to 35 million.
- The average teen is spending more than $100 a week. About two-thirds of that is money they can spend however they wish; the rest is for specific items, such as bus fares and school lunches.

These sound like huge numbers, and they are. Young people in the United States spend more than the total populations of some small countries do. In fact, they have the spending power of a country on its own.

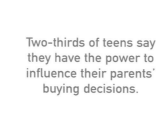

Two-thirds of teens say they have the power to influence their parents' buying decisions.

Pester power

Young Americans have learned the art of persuasion, it seems. More than two-thirds of teens say they have the power to influence their parents' buying decisions.

And they twist them around their little fingers. Researchers have repeatedly found that parents hate saying no to teens. They're more likely to go without something themselves than deny their children.

The number of young U.S. consumers is expected to reach 35 million by 2010.

Budgeting: getting it right!

Budgeting is the simplest form of money management. It's not the most exciting part; in fact, spending, and even saving, beat budgeting by a long shot! But it's one of those things that gets easier (once you've done it). Budgeting is like going to the dentist. It's a tough call, but you know it's doing you good!

Making a budget means you recognize that your money supply is limited—and that's not fun! It almost certainly means that you want to do lots of things you know you may not be able to afford—and that's not fun either. Above all, budgets require self-discipline—and that may or may not be fun, depending on your personality!

The good news about budgeting is that once your budget is drawn up, it'll keep you from worrying about whatever spending you're going to do. And that should make it all worthwhile! A budget will almost certainly show you that there IS enough money to do the things you want. You may have to save over time to achieve them, even wait a little. You may have to buy something in parts—your CD collection, for example, or a winter outfit!

Money Planner

Budgeting is part of money management.
Draw up a budget for the week or month.

Income
Make four columns in a notebook, and write down your weekly allowance amount in the left-hand column. This is the income column. You can add to this column if you receive money from somewhere else. Only count the money you get regularly and can rely on.

income	needs	luxury	saving

Expenditures
Needs: In the second column, write down your expenditures. That's the money you know you're going to have to spend.
Luxuries: The third column is for the things you want—as opposed to those you need—for example, the necessary copy of *Fluffy Bunnies Monthly.*

Balancing
When you've done that, total the two expenditure columns and see if this sum compares to your income.

Saving
In the fourth column list the things you want to save for. If there's anything left over, write this in your savings column. If not, go down the luxuries list and cut out enough to give you cash to save.

It's not always easy to put off doing something you want to do, or buying something you think you need. We live in a world of promises. Get it now—pay later! Put it on your credit card. Worry about it when the bill turns up!

If you go along with this approach, you'll almost certainly suffer from bad budgeting habits. You may get someone to help you out because you're young or you don't know any better—but unfortunately, this will change. In the real world, the only people who'll help you out may well want a lot of money to do so.

Piggy banks

In earlier times, in Western societies, a pig was a kind of poor man's money box. A piglet, bought from the market in spring, could live on household leftovers, and would be fattened up and ready for the butcher just before winter. Your piggy bank, which is fed on leftovers of your money, fattens in the same way, and can be smashed to pieces when it's full.

In German-speaking countries, it was the custom to give apprentices—young people who were training to become craftsmen—a pig as a reward for a year's work. The pig, therefore, became the symbol of investing—both with money and in young people!

Early piggy banks

Some say piggy banks were used in Bali, Indonesia, more than 1,500 years ago. The pottery piggy bank in Europe is much more recent—it was first made around 1500.

Clay pyggs

No one is too sure about the true history of the piggy bank, but most people believe that it gets its name from the orange clay called pygg, from which it was originally made. In the Middle Ages, people throughout Europe stored items such as salt in wide-necked jars, which were made from pygg clay.

The so-called pig jar retained its name long after potters stopped using pygg clay to produce pottery.

Money was also kept in the jars and by the early 1700s, the jars had been given the name of pig banks, from which followed the present name of piggy bank.

Mr. Micawber's wisdom

Mr. Micawber is a well-known character from one of Charles Dickens' books. This British author wrote many novels about life in the 1800s, when people who got into debt had a really hard time!

An annual income that is greater than annual expenditures produces happiness.

According to Mr. Micawber, the way to stay out of debt was to balance your books—to the penny!

An annual income that is less than annual expenditures produces misery.

That is how Mr. Micawber felt when he lectured his young clerk, David Copperfield, in Dickens' famous novel of the same name.

(By the way, Mr. Micawber was a guy who didn't practice what he preached—so he ended up in a debtor's prison!)

Rationing

Smart about money

It's 1940, and it's wartime in Britain, France, Italy, and Belgium. In fact, most of Europe is at war. And being at war leads to all kinds of cutbacks. Money is badly needed to fund the war, so the government stops spending on things made abroad. At the same time, factories at home have stopped making luxury goods and are making war machines. Ships at sea are in danger from enemy warships and submarines, and planes are being shot down in large numbers. It's time to tighten the belt!

As food stocks run down, the government introduces rationing. From now on, everyone will be rationed to receive a share of what's available. It's no good having money. That won't buy you extras. What you need now are ration coupons.

Each person in the country is issued a ration book with a certain number of coupons to buy butter, meat, tea, cheese, jam, eggs, and sweets.

If you use up all your ration coupons on a big shopping trip, there won't be any more, so you have to budget. Clothes are rationed, too. Each man, woman, and child has 66 coupons a year. A man's suit uses up 26 of these and a lady's dress about 11. Using your ration coupons won't do much to make you look smart, but you'll certainly learn to think smart.

There shouldn't be any need to go back to rationing to convince you that putting something away for a rainy day is far smarter than blowing it all on day one. Apart from not being very clever, it's completely unrealistic. For most of your life you'll need to earn the money you spend, and that's going to involve hard work. And paying for necessities, your living expenses, will eat into your earnings big-time. So getting into the habit of managing your spending early on makes sense. Emergencies will always crop up—but you'll be able to cope.

A basic guideline:
- Put 30 percent of your money into a savings account, and watch it grow
- Donate 10 percent to charity, or a person or organization that will really benefit from your help
- Spend the rest!

Everyone will have different ideas and priorities. If your money is money you have earned, you will almost certainly be able to set your own guidelines. But if it's an allowance—pocket money given to you by your parents—they may want to have their say! They'll have good reasons, so it's wise to listen.

All you can have this week, Ma'am!

4 oz. bacon and ham (that's 4 slices)

8 oz. sugar

2 oz. butter (enough to butter half a loaf)

8 oz. cooking fat

a small portion of meat (not much!)

2 oz. tea (enough to make 4 cups)

1 oz. cheese (enough for 1 sandwich)

2 oz. jam (enough for 4 slices of toast)

Debt

It may seem odd to confront you with the hazards of debt when you're still earning small bucks or just getting pocket money. But this isn't to advise you on the here and now so much as to make you aware of the consequences of what may happen later on. Too often people are plunged into debt because they believed one scam or another, or because they just didn't realize how difficult things might become once they were in debt. So, if you're aware right now of what happens when you get into debt, you might just think twice about drifting down that route in the future.

" Money is better than poverty, if only for financial reasons."

Woody Allen

Debt is not a word any of us likes. We obviously associate it with trouble and not being able to pay for things. But debt only means that we owe somebody money. In fact, most people are in debt. Anyone who has a house and pays a mortgage is in debt.

So why does debt have such a bad name? And is it a good thing or a bad thing to be in debt? After all, attitudes have changed, and we're always being encouraged to buy now and pay later.

Legalities

There are technical problems, too. The company or companies you owe money to, called creditors, can have your name blacklisted with credit bureaus or agencies. They put your credit details into a report that is available to banks, lending companies, and businesses. Once you have a bad credit report, you might have trouble getting credit from anyone until the report is cleared. This may take years.

In the worst case, a company may refer you for legal action. This may result in a court judgment that forces you to pay back the amount owed over a fixed period of time. It may also result in debt collectors knocking at your door and taking your personal possessions away to be sold. It all seems pretty harsh, but the best way to avoid all of this, of course, is not to get into debt in the first place.

Payback time

Debt doesn't become a problem until you're not able to pay it back. This is the part that needs to be avoided at all costs, even if it does mean doing without the things you want. In the end, being OUT of debt may be the only thing you long for.

The consequences of being in debt can be pretty grim. You worry about it all the time. You can't spend what you want. All of your spare money goes into paying off the charges or interest that's mounting on the debt. You can't see the end of it.

A helping hand

There are people around who can help you with debt management. They'll deal with your creditors for you and try to arrange repayment at a rate you can afford. They'll also advise you about your rights. It's not always legal to hassle people over minor debts.

There are also companies that loan you the money to pay off all of your debts so you have just one "affordable" payment to make. This sounds fine, but it simply means you pay over a much longer period of time—and pay more interest. Such help needs to be looked at carefully by someone who can guide you.

"I've been rich, and I've been poor. Rich is better."

Sophie Tucker

Surprise money

It's always great when you're surprised with a gift of money. You might get a small thrill from finding a coin in the gutter or from unearthing a shoe box of cash on a garbage dump. Odds are that both these things won't come your way! But (surprise, surprise!) there might be a stash of cash with your name on it right now, or coming your way sometime in the future, that could change your life.

Birthday cash

You may have been given money for your birthday by fond relatives—perhaps you even received money when you were born, in which case your parents may have already opened a bank or savings account in your name. Could your parents have been putting money away into an account for years and have forgotten to tell you about it?

Savings bonds are also given as presents. These are simply notes that promise to pay you all of your money back, with interest, after a certain number of years.

Trust funds

Your parents may even have established a trust fund for you. Sometimes grown-ups set up trust funds at a bank or financial company where money is invested until such time as their children are to have access to it for themselves. Usually, an age is established before which the funds cannot be touched.

Inheritance

A sad way to get money is to inherit it when a person dies. A will is a legal document that says how a person's assets will be distributed after his or her death. If no will exists, a dead person is said to be intestate, and laws have to be used to decide the list of heirs. You might still inherit, but a stranger might decide just what you get!

Inheritance tax

If a great deal of money is left in a will, the government may claim an inheritance tax. Inheriting stuff can be emotional, especially if it's from someone close to you. It's usually best to put your money into a bank, where it can be earning interest while you decide what to do with it. When you're ready, you can use it to buy something you really want.

Grants

You might someday apply for a grant—a sum of money intended to help pay for your education, for some related activity like a school trip, or to learn a special musical or artistic skill. Grants usually state quite clearly how the money can and can't be used, but it's worth finding out about grant funds because you might well be able to apply for some.

Windfalls

It goes without saying that if any of these windfalls come to you, they should be used wisely. If you have money in savings bonds, or trust funds, or bank accounts, or anything else, you have what are called assets. And assets establish your net worth. The older you get, the more important your net worth will be to you. It will get you financial help from the bank to buy your dream purchase, to help you through college, or to fund that around-the-world student trip.

The male line

Some countries only allow male heirs to inherit. The sons get everything! This is called patrilineal inheritance. Then again, in some cultures only females can inherit—matrilineal inheritance.

When everything goes to the eldest child, it's called primogeniture. In many countries that have a ruling monarch—like Britain, Spain, or Japan, for example—the crown is passed down this way: always to the eldest child, whether male or female.

In other countries it is law that all inheritance must be shared evenly between all the children. This happens in France. It's not always a good idea. If a French farmer dies, for example, his land may be cut into equal parts, one for each child. When the children die, the land gets carved up even more. In time, the plots of land will be too small to be worth farming.

Chinese red packets

A "red packet" is simply a red envelope with money in it, often decorated with lucky symbols, which symbolizes luck and wealth. It's called *Hong Bao* in Chinese. Traditionally, red packets are handed out to children by their parents, grandparents, relatives, and even close neighbors and friends during Chinese New Year. They're also popular gifts for weddings and birthdays. You might even be given one by your grateful boss as an end-of-year bonus.

How much you get in your red packet depends on age. Usually the older you are, the more money you get. A 5-year-old might receive $1 or $2, but a 15-year-old should get enough to buy something really exciting.

The Magic moneybag

Here's an old tale from Korea about a couple who got lucky—but when they pushed their luck, things went swiftly backward. The moral is clear—don't get greedy when someone gives you a surprise gift. Or is it that money comes and goes—while real values don't? What do YOU think?

Once, in Korea, there lived a couple who were poor. They lived in a straw hut. Each day they would cut two bundles of firewood, one for themselves and one to sell for food. The couple worked hard every day until their labors came to the attention of the gods. The husband was called to heaven and told that since the couple was so diligent and hardworking they'd be rewarded.

The man was surprised to be given an empty moneybag that he was told to open once a day. And, sure enough, each day when the bag was opened it held one piece of silver.

Soon the couple had a stack of silver pieces.

"Let's buy an ox or some land," said the farmer.

"No, what I want is a house of bricks," replied his wife.

But the money ran out before the house was finished.

"We need more money. I need to open the bag more often."

So the man opened the bag a second time that day and a second piece of silver fell out. He did it a third time with the same result. But on the fourth

opening, no silver came. Not only that, the house had completely disappeared.

"You see!" said the farmer. "We can't depend on a magic moneybag from heaven. Let's go back to cutting firewood. It's a more reliable way."

And from that day on, they led their old, hardworking, but happy life.

Borrowing

However hard you try to manage your budget, there are always going to be times when you need that extra amount. One of the key problems with running out of money when you really need it, is that you have to ask someone to help. You have to find someone to LEND you money, and you have to BORROW it on terms that are not too stringent.

From friends

Friends are more likely than anyone else to help you out with a loan—an interest-free loan! In other words, they'll lend you money to be repaid, dollar for dollar. Having said that, any loan, whatever generosity lies behind it, is a debt. And debts have a nasty habit of turning sour. While you owe money to friends, you may get asked to help them out with favors and, of course, it's difficult to say no.

Above all, remember that even if the loan is quite casual, it is a loan and not a gift. Friendships often fall apart when borrowers forget their obligations.

From parents

Borrowing from your parents can be as casual as borrowing from a friend—but not always. Depending on the amount of the loan, you'll need to negotiate how much and how often you make repayments. And bear in mind, there will be no further loans or helping handouts if you get this wrong. Parents may not be willing to give you a second chance, and it wouldn't be wise of them to do so. If you're old enough to borrow from them in the first place, you're certainly old enough to take responsibility for the repayments.

And parents might just charge interest—not necessarily in money terms, but they'll be bound to ask for those extra chores and courtesies while you're in their debt.

From companies

Special companies known as finance companies lend money, too. They often charge higher interest than the banks, but if you don't have a high enough credit rating at the bank, you may be forced to turn elsewhere. You may also find there are age restrictions on borrowing from these companies.

From banks

If you really can't get or don't want a loan from your friends or family, or if you need a great deal of money, then you'll probably find yourself at the bank. You'll find you won't be able to start without some financial help, and borrowing from a bank will be one way to overcome this. Just be very clear about the terms of borrowing, especially when larger sums are involved and when the lender is a financial institution like a bank.

Credit rating

If you have already opened a bank account at your local branch, you will have some history with them and you may be eligible for an overdraft, or a loan. Even so, you won't get either if you're not considered to be financially responsible. To assess this, the bank gives you what's known as a credit rating. They look at your reason for wanting the cash, your income or income forecast, and your record of deposits and withdrawals from your account. You may find they ask for a guarantor—a parent or other grown-up who will guarantee to repay the loan if you default. In this case, you'll have to convince your guarantor AND the bank.

Overdrafts and loans

Overdrafts and loans cover you when you spend more money than you have in your account—up to an agreed limit. You'll pay interest on the borrowed money and maybe also a small upfront fee.

Shylock

William Shakespeare, the great English playwright of the late 1500s and early 1600s, wrote a play called *The Merchant of Venice*. Although it's one of his most popular plays, it tells a dark and unhappy story.

Antonio was a merchant who lived in the city of Venice in Italy. One day, his friend Bassanio asked him for a loan of 3,000 ducats. Bassanio planned to use the money to court the beautiful and wealthy Lady Portia of Belmont.

Antonio didn't have the money, so he suggested they visit a moneylender called Shylock. Shylock was despised by the people, who called him a dog and even spat upon him. He, in turn, hated the Venetians, especially the merchant Antonio, who lent money free of charge.

But the three met and agreed on a deal. Antonio could have the money for three months. But if he failed to repay it, Shylock would claim a pound of flesh cut from Antonio's body in return. This was his revenge for being so ill-treated.

Bassanio got his loan and married Portia. But in the meantime, Antonio's merchant ships were lost at sea and he couldn't raise the 3,000 ducats to pay back Shylock. This meant certain death.

So, at the end of three months, Shylock brought Antonio to court to claim his pound of flesh. But no one knew that Bassanio's new and clever wife, Portia, had disguised herself as the judge.

She agreed that Shylock could have the pound of flesh he claimed—but no more and no less. He wasn't allowed to spill even one drop of Antonio's blood or he himself would die.

So Shylock's plot to kill Antonio was foiled, and for his greed, he was ordered to pay half his money to the government and half to Antonio. Shylock's desire for revenge had ruined him.

Earning money

It isn't long before you begin to understand that the most reliable way of getting money is to earn it. Your pocket money or allowance may already come with strings attached—the occasional household chore for a dollar or two. But joining the labor market —selling your time, effort, and expertise outside the home—not only brings in the cash but gets you a lot more benefits as well.

Fitting it in

Your first job will almost certainly be running alongside schoolwork. Don't underestimate the demands. If you take on work, you will need to be committed to it for the time it takes. Work will need to be a priority just like school is. Added to this, you won't want to give up your sports activities or your social or family life. So fitting it all in will take extra doses of energy and organization. Make sure you've thought this all out before you take the leap.

The benefits

For a start, working in a job is a whole new experience. Whether you work for someone else, or set up a business and work for yourself, you're going to be moving in a new environment, working with new people, and learning new skills. All of this is great preparation for the real thing—when you leave school and enter the adult work market.

There's another plus. If you haven't decided on a career path, then deciding what job to take on could be a bit of a lottery. By trying different jobs now, before you leave school, you'll get a feel for some of what's available and whether you're cut out for it.

Finally, you'll be earning money that rewards your effort and contribution— and that should make you feel good! You should get a real sense of personal accomplishment and a confidence boost!

The best job for you

The best job for you is the one you like doing and in which you can demonstrate some expertise. The jobs available may require lots of muscle—stacking shelves, making deliveries, or packing in a warehouse, for example. Jobs like this often involve working outdoors, and this may be appealing. Or, you may opt for what's known as a desk job—involving more brainpower than muscle power.

Whatever kind of job you decide to look for, a good way to start is by listing your skills and interests.

Which are your favorite subjects at school?
☐ English ☐ Science ☐ Foreign languages ☐ Social studies
☐ Math ☐ Art ☐ Sports

Do you prefer to work by yourself or with a group? [   ]
What are your hobbies out of school? [   ]
What chores do you do at home?
Happily [   ] Fairly happily [   ] Unhappily [   ]
Do you like looking after other people's property?
☐ Houses ☐ Gardens ☐ Pets ☐ Children
Do you want a safe job or do you long for a challenge, even an adventure? [   ]
Do you want to work indoors or outdoors? [   ]
Are you practical and inventive, especially with your hands? [   ]
What do you want to do as a career? [   ]
What do you think you do best? [   ]

Are you ...
☐ Neat? ☐ Punctual? ☐ Cheerful? ☐ Reliable?
Do you like to take responsibility or be told what to do?

You can be as honest as you like because this isn't a real application. You are interviewing YOU. Looking at your answers will at least help you to figure out what you don't want to do—and what you do!

Employment law

Most governments limit the age at which young people can start work, especially in certain jobs that require handling machinery or working in a dangerous environment. The kind of jobs that might be off-limits are mining, working with power-driven saws or cutting blades, excavating, roofing or demolition, driving a motor vehicle, and jobs serving alcohol in a store, bar, or restaurant, for example. You'll also find that the number of hours you are legally permitted to work is limited, or that you can only work within certain times of day. These laws can vary from place to place, so it's best to find out for yourself.

Whatever you do, don't go into a job knowing that you'll be breaking the law. It just isn't worth it!

Social security

Unfortunately, it doesn't end here. You must also make a payment to the government department responsible for making payments to you when you retire from work.

From the time you start earning, you will be given a Social Security number that you will need throughout your life for all kinds of things. With Social Security, you will be paying a fixed contribution each month.

And, once again, it's the law and not something you can pretend you don't know about.

Taxes

Taxes are moneys that are collected by governments and local authorities so they can provide all the services we want—roads, bridges, schools, libraries, police forces, garbage collection, parks, and so on.

There are also taxes on things we buy, like houses, cars, and goods in the stores. If you earn money, either working for someone else or on your own, your income will be taxed.

If you're working for someone else, they'll deduct tax from your earnings before you receive them. If you're working for yourself, you will have a legal responsibility to pay these taxes. And you won't be able to escape this, so this isn't a chapter you can skip! Just because we like all the things that taxes buy, it doesn't mean that we like paying taxes. It's difficult to hand over your hard-earned money to the government—but it's the law. Forget to pay your taxes and you can end up with a hefty fine! Taxes are serious business!

However, you might just escape if you're young and not earning much. If you're only working outside school hours, you're unlikely to earn more than your personal allowance. This is a sum that is always changing—and it's tax free.

Being employed

One of the best ways of getting work experience is to work for someone else. Even if you have plans to get your own business as soon as you can, it's still a good way to learn the ropes—and get paid for it.

Whether you work in an office, a store, or a car wash, most businesses are run to make money. Just watching and learning how other people do it will give you valuable knowledge to draw on later.

The workplace
First, the workplace. This will be laid out to house a specific job or set of jobs. The staffers will have access to the equipment they need without taking a long walk around the building. There will be bathroom facilities, safety exits, and enough light for workers to see what they're doing. And they'll be warm in winter. There are laws about how hot and cold the workplace can be.

The staff
The staff will already be trained to do their jobs, or, like you, they may be trained on the job. In this case, someone will be monitoring their progress and helping them along. Each member of the staff may have a different task. Is there a job here that interests you—that you might like to take up as a career? If so, try to work alongside this person or talk to him or her about the job.

The equipment
Everyone who handles equipment will be trained to use it. There will be someone available to maintain or repair it, upgrade it, or buy new equipment, as needed.

The job
When you take a job, you enter into a contract. This states that you will work in return for a sum of money—your paycheck. If you don't work, your employer has no obligation to pay you. But this is someone you'll want to impress. They may well be able to help you to be successful later on. But even if this isn't the case, your employer deserves your full effort and commitment.

The pay
You may be paid weekly or monthly, depending on the system in place. You may also get paid cash, or by check or electronic transfer. In both these latter cases you will need to have set up your own bank account before you can receive anything.

Remember that checks and transfers can take three to four days to clear into your account, so your wage isn't there the day it's paid.

And remember: your pay is often agreed to as a gross sum; that is a full amount, taking no account of the deductions that will have to be made. The net amount is what you will actually see: the gross amount less taxes and Social Security contributions.

Applying for work

Finding work

- Scan the job ads.
- Visit the local employment agencies.
- Look on notice boards in local stores.
- Ask at the reception desk in targeted offices and companies.
- Put the word out among friends and grown-ups.

Writing an application

- Send a letter and a resumé.
- Fill in the application form, as provided.
- Keep this short and to the point—and check the spelling.
- Address the envelope clearly.

Attach your resumé

- Your resumé should list your accomplishments.
- Start with your name, address, and contact details.
- State your age, education, and any exam passed and qualifications earned to date.
- List your membership in clubs and organizations.
- List your interests and hobbies.
- List references—people who know you well and who can write a short letter to say what a wonderful employee you'd make. The teacher of your best subject at school would be a good choice! (Sorry—best friends or doting parents won't do.)

Go for an interview

- Look smart and clean.
- Be prepared—find out something about the company and the job before you get there, even if it's not much.
- Have at least one question ready for the moment you're asked if you have one—it will come!
- Arrive punctually.
- Be yourself!

Talk the Biz!

Minimum wage

Minimum wage is the smallest amount of money that certain employees should be paid per hour. In the United States, both the federal government and state governments set the minimum wage. In 1938, the federal government passed the Fair Labor Standards Act, which established a minimum wage. The minimum wage then was just 25 cents per hour! Today, the federal minimum wage is $5.15 per hour.

Gross

A gross sum is the full sum received or owed, without any deductions or charges taken from it.

Net

The gross sum LESS any deductions and charges leaves the net sum.

Saying good-bye

Remember that you have not sold your soul or your happiness to anyone. If the job doesn't work out, if it's boring, too difficult, not what you expected, too tiring, or if you feel threatened or unsafe in any way, remember that you don't have to stay. You may not be able to walk out at once. You may have to give notice of a few days or two weeks.

Always try to discuss such problems with your employer before you leave. There are often ways around these kinds of problems, and you should always stick with something if you possibly can. Your resumé will record all your work experience for future employers, and it doesn't look good if you've had three jobs in four months!

Directory of possible jobs

	Job description	Details	Expenses	Help/Advice	Research
In office	Coffee person	Making coffee for staff	Coffee pot	Make a tour of office buildings and visit each office. You'll only be able to cater for a few, though.	
	Office gofer	Doing odd jobs, running errands	None	Be ready to do anything without complaining.	
	Call-a-kid	Organizing kids to do office work	Telephone, notepads	Use your organizational skills to draw up a list of kids who you can rely on to work when you want them to.	Read about office management and keeping records.
	Newspaper recycler	Collecting old papers, magazines for recycling	Paper bags	Find out where recycling stations are before you start. It may be in your local supermarket.	
	Envelope stuffer	Filling envelopes for drops, mailings, etc.	None	You can do this at home or in the office.	
	Filing clerk	Putting documents in filing cabinets, etc.	None	Normally a full-time job, so look for small companies that may need part-time help.	
	Mail runner	Taking mail to post office	None	You can do this after school, since that's when mail is sent.	Make sure you know your area well.
	Mail room worker	Collecting, sorting mail, stamping, etc.	None	This can be a full-time job for holidays or Christmas.	
In factory	Can collector	Collecting cans for recycling	Garbage bags	Locate the recycling center or bin. It may be in your local supermarket.	
	Cafeteria help	Doing dishes		Ask parents if you can try their place of work.	Locate factories, etc., with cafeterias.
	Equipment Cleaner	Cleaning machines when not in use	Buckets, cleaning liquid, sponge	This can be done after-hours when machines are not working.	
	Sweeper	Clearing leaves in parking lots, etc.	Brush and rake	This is an autumn job that companies often forget.	
	Cake, cookie seller	Selling homemade cookies and cakes	Baking ingredients	People love homemade snacks at break times.	Find out how long it will take you to prepare your daily output.
	Menu printer	Printing menus for cafeteria	Computer, card or paper	Offer to create easy-to-read, brightly colored material.	
In store	Sign painter	Painting sale signs, messages, etc., on store windows	Correct paint brushes and stencils	Make sure you use a paint that rubs off. Sales don't go on forever.	
	Bagger	Bagging purchased items in supermarkets	None	Supermarkets often use baggers to help shoppers.	
	Messenger	Delivering mail, sold articles, etc.	Bicycle	Stores have to get stuff from place to place. Make cards to advertise what you do and give them to stores.	
	Shelver	Stacking shelves	None	This job can be done at any time of the day, so it is good for after school.	Find busy stores to approach.
	Laundry help	Helping in laundromat		Laundromats are another place to find work in the evening or on weekends.	
In restaurant	Dishwasher	Washing dishes		All restaurants need dishwashers, so just keep trying until you find one that needs you.	
	Vegetable peeler	Preparing, cleaning vegetables	None	The vegetables used in restaurants have to be washed and peeled. Someone has to do it.	

Working for yourself
young entrepreneur

When you start looking for a job, there are always two ways to go: to work for others, helping them make a success of their business and enjoying the security of paid employment; or to go it alone. This takes guts. It's not a scheme for the faint-hearted since it takes a high dose of risk, effort, and optimism. It takes a spirit of enterprise.

But for many this is a natural move. The way people work in employment is changing the world over. In your grandparents' day, people expected to keep their jobs for most of their lives. They may have started in a job at 18 and retired from the same company well past their 60s. Today, young people know they will need to make many career moves and may even want to be part of the growing armies of freelance operators working outside companies and not within.

The dictionary will tell you that an entrepreneur is a person who organizes and manages a business, taking on both the risk and the profit. What this means is that an entrepreneur finds a business opportunity, creates a business plan of how it can be set up and operated, gets it underway, manages it—and receives any profit that it makes. You have some good role models:

Richard Branson, founder of Virgin

Bill Gates, co-founder of Microsoft

Anita Roddick, founder of the Body Shop

Go for it!

Today, there are young entrepreneurs in the thousands, setting up on their own and promoting their own wares successfully. Young people are often highly innovative and independent, and soon find they are enjoying all the rewards, excitement, and job satisfaction of running their own business.

More questions ...

- Are you the right age to carry the business you want to do? There may be legal restrictions, so be sure to find out.
- Is it the right time of year to start your business? If not, should you wait?
- Do you need any money to get started? If so, how much? Do you have it or can you borrow it?
- Do you need any equipment to carry out your business idea? If so, do you have it or can you hire or borrow it?
- Will your business idea make money or be lots of effort for nothing?

If you're doubtful about any of these questions, you need to ask for advice—and your parents will almost certainly be the best people to broach the subject with. If there's some borrowing to do, they may well be the ones to help you out.

Then again ...

Choosing what you do in your business and who your customers are, deciding how you will find them, service them, and charge them—all these are hugely demanding. You might well decide it's best to give self-employment a pass, at least until you've gained a little more experience in the workplace.

Business ideas

You're well on your way to knowing exactly what you're going to do. But there's one last, important step—your business plan. This is the plan that will help you achieve your goals. You wouldn't set off on a vacation without knowing where you were going, booking travel and accommodations, and packing the right clothes. And you shouldn't set off on a business venture without the same kind of knowledge.

Your business name

Come up with something catchy that inspires you, perhaps even catches the mood of the venture—and something your customers will remember.

Your service

You need to know exactly what service you are offering. You also need to know what you aren't.

Your service cost

Decide how much you will charge to be ahead of the competition, since there are others out there with a similar service.

Your requirements

Skills: Do you need to learn new skills? If so, do you have to spend money, or is studying the key?

Equipment: Do you need equipment—a computer or lawn mower or other tools of the trade?

Advertising: How will you promote your business so people know you're out there?

Your goals

Your goals can be short-term or long-term, but they should be realistic. They'll help motivate you. If you set goals that are too high, it'll be easy to get frustrated.

What it takes to be an entrepreneur

Passion
Are you totally passionate about your business idea? Do you absolutely believe in the service you are providing? And, once you've got your venture up and running—do you have the passion and the energy to keep going?

Innovation
Entrepreneurs are highly innovative and creative individuals with the vision and insight to spot opportunities and act upon them. They have the ability to carve out a new niche in a market where others might not have seen it—and turn ideas into a solid business.

Commitment
Do you have the commitment and determination to make your venture a success? Planning, setting up, and running a business requires a lot of hard work. Your friends and leisure activities may have to take a back seat from time to time.

Courage
A successful entrepreneur is prepared to make big decisions and take on tough challenges.

Ability to set goals
An entrepreneur will set specific and realistic goals and have a clear plan of how to achieve these. Your venture won't be a success if you don't do this, because you won't have specific targets to aim for or measure your performance against.

Sound judgment
Contrary to popular belief, you don't have to be a high risk-taker to be a successful entrepreneur. It's more about knowing which risks to take—and when you should take them. You will also have to judge what needs your attention at a certain time and what doesn't.

Flexibility
An entrepreneur has to be flexible. Will you be able to cope with the different roles and responsibilities? Flexibility also means recognizing changes that may be needed if things aren't going according to plan—and learning from experiences (both good and bad).

Independence
One of the main reasons for starting a business is the desire to be your own boss. Entrepreneurs want to be in charge of their own destiny.

Leadership skills
Once you have built up a team around you, your staff will be looking to you for strong leadership. This means setting realistic goals, being honest, and taking responsibility for your actions.

Service jobs

There are just two basic kinds of businesses: those that make and sell a product, and those that provide a service. Here are two services that you might try.

Babysitting

Every busy parent needs a good babysitter from time to time. If you enjoy being around small children, this job might be for you. If you decide to babysit, you should sign up for a class that teaches infant and toddler care. Many times these classes also teach CPR for infants and children. This is important to learn in case there is an emergency while you are babysitting.

Lawn mowing

Grass always grows and lawns need to be mowed. A lawn mowing venture can be a great way for a young person to start out in the business world. If you decide to mow lawns, you will need to find a mower you can use. It is important to have an adult show you how to properly run and handle a mower before you begin. The best lawns to mow are those that are near you, unless you have a vehicle and trailer to haul your mower around. Remember, mowers can be dangerous, so always use caution when operating one.

Investing

Once you earn some money, you might want to invest it. Of course, some people would say that doing things with your money is always a risk. After all, how many times do you buy something that doesn't work, or isn't exactly what you want, or is just a waste of money? But when you decide to invest your money, you are most certainly running the risk of getting less back than you put in, or even losing your money altogether.

Of course, this is not what investors plan on doing. They plan to gain from the risk. And they anticipate that the gain will be far greater than if they were saving their money somewhere safe—in a bank account, for example.

Investing in stocks and shares is open to anyone. Depending on who and what you invest in, you should be able to keep your risk to a minimum by doing your homework and spreading the risk among lots of investments rather than just one.

Talk the Biz!

USP
Refer to the special qualities in your service as your USP—your unique selling point.

Bottom line
You hear this phrase a lot when people are talking about business. "What's your bottom line?" What they want to know is whether you're making a profit or a loss, and by how much.

Niche market
This is YOUR piece of the market opportunity. It's the part of the market that you can claim as your own—and you will have gotten it because there are things about YOUR business that your customers can't get elsewhere.

Directory of self-employment jobs

Job description	Details	Do your research!	Funding needed/ setup costs	License /legal	Presentation/ helpful advice	Watch the competition
Household						
Garage cleaner	Sweep out, tidy tools, stack boxes, etc.	Ask owners how they want things arranged	Bucket, cleaning tools	None	Make sure you do a good job so you get invited back	Find out what other cleaners charge
Spring cleaner	Seasonal in many places		Cleaning equipment, brushes, cloth, sprays	None	Be careful with clients' stuff. A broken vase or mirror might lose you a job	
Painter of garden furniture/fences	Seasonal	Try out on an old fence or chair	Paint, brushes	None	Wear the right clothing, since you're sure to get paint on you	See what products others use
Gardening	Seasonal	Work with a pro for free	Gardening tools if not provided	None	Bring tools if you're not sure the client has any	
Car wash	Inside and out, also wax and polish	Find the right products for the job	Bucket, soap, wax	None	Always use car soap	
Snow shoveler	Seasonal		Snow shovel	None	Remember to keep snow off the road as much as possible	
Window cleaning	Clean windows outside house and inside		Bucket, ladder, cleaning liquid, sponges, etc.	None	Offer a regular service at a competitive price	See if you're quicker than the competition
Sports						
General helper	Weekly clubs often need assistance		None	None	You could do anything from cleaning to handing out tickets and equipment	
Golf caddie	For private golfers	Watch a professional caddie at work	Calling card	None	When you begin, watch other caddies and ask questions. Make sure you're big enough to carry the bag!	
Equipment manager	Cleaning and looking after sports equipment		Elbow grease	None	Begin with school teams and ask around	
Entertainment						
Party entertainer	Clown, magician, balloon artist, storytelling, acting, music making—there are lots of opportunities here	Try to watch an adult working or read as much as you can about the activity	A suitable costume, books to read, musical instrument	None	Make sure you're confident in what you're doing. Remember, you're performing and people will be watching. Rehearse well so you feel good doing it	
Photographer's assistant	For special occasions or portrait work	Visit a studio or watch a few weddings	Camera and film	None	If you're at a function, dress for it. Never look sloppy or untidy	See how much a pro charges and charge less
Musician, DJ	For events or teaching	CDs, records, two CD or record players, stereo set-up & microphone	None	None	Make sure you have the transportation that will carry all your equipment. Always arrive early to set up	
Animals						
Pet sitting/dog walking	Looking after pets while owners are away	Which local families are too busy to walk dogs	Pair of stout walking shoes or boots	None	Be sure you like animals and can handle them if they behave badly	
Riding school helper	Shoveling out and cleaning tack		Boots	None	You may be able to get free rides rather than money as payment	
Animal shelter worker	Helping clean kennels, walking dogs, feeding		Boots	None	If you like animals and there is a zoo close by, you could do the same kinds of jobs there	
Modeling						
Art school model	Modeling for students		None	None	Contact colleges that teach art and offer to be an artist's model	
Photo agency model	Modeling for commercials		Makeup, photos of yourself	None	Look in the ad columns for agencies that supply models and contact them	

Selling services

Directory of self-employment jobs

Job description	Details	Do your research!	Funding needed/ setup costs	License /Legal	Presentation/ helpful advice	Watch the competition
Family						
Babysitter	Run a group to make the most of this opportunity	List families with young children	Telephone	Check age	Make sure the people who work for you are as reliable as you are	
Adopt a granny/ grandpa	Weekly visits and help with cleaning, shopping, etc.	Find out what jobs the elderly find difficult	Variable, depending on jobs	None	Take time to make friends with your adopted grandparents	
Plant sitter/house guard	For absent homeowners	Who is going on vacation?	Flashlight, key ring, labels	None	Label house keys	
Birthday party organizer	Organization service, food and entertainment	Read books on party organization	Variable, depending on what is expected of you	None	Find out well in advance what your client wants you to do. Always clean up after the party	See what other organizers offer
Deliveries						
Paper route	Delivering papers	Find out what papers are delivered	Bicycle may be needed and strong carrier sack	Age limits	Put papers where customers can get them without getting wet	
Flier delivery	Delivering fliers		Carrier sack if not supplied	Age limits	Get a flier from someone, find out where it came from, and ask if he needs more help	
Computer						
Card and sign maker	Making cards, signs for garage sales, etc.		Computer, printer, correct size cards	None	Make your own attractive cards to advertise what you do	
Online salesperson	Sell articles of clothing, toys, etc., online	Watch somebody selling online before you try	Computer, site setup cost	None	Learn to pinpoint items that are popular or sell quickly	
Computer consultant	Help for those who don't know computers		Computer	None	Understand your software programs so you can answer questions quickly	
Desktop publisher	Publish newsletters, fliers, menus	See how existing materials are laid out and designed	Computer, printer, paper, card, ink	None	Look for work at school, in churches, retirement homes, cafeterias, etc.	See how competition lays out work
Essay, report typist	Type essays, reports, or manuscripts		Computer, paper	None	Must be quick at keyboard and good at grammar, spelling, etc.	
Sales						
Plant sales	Grow herbs in small pots	Try chives, mint, parsley, basil, dill, coriander	Pots, compost, potting tools	Sales permit	Popular with restaurants and cooks at home, where good herbs make good money and can be harvested time and again	
Old clothes/toy sales	Selling old clothes, toys, games, etc.	A selection of articles to sell— no cost		None	Sell toys and games you haven't used for ages. Set up a stand or go to nurseries	
Sandwiches, refreshment sales	Selling sandwiches, etc.	Test market to see what is popular	Baking equipment, fillings, juice, water	Sales permit	Specialize in just a couple of items and do them well. Two kinds of sandwiches or cookies	Check prices offered by competition
Make and do						
Decorative objects, handicrafts	Selling your own creations		Material, fabrics, etc.	Sales permit	Easter and Christmas decorations sell well, as do soft toys	
T-shirt design	Design and sell T-shirts		T-shirts, fabric paints, brushes, sequins	Sales permit	Find out what designs are popular. Advertise by wearing your design	
Stuffed toys	Selling stuffed toys		Stuffing, fabric, sewing material	Sales permit	As well as animals you can make larger, stuffed pillow animals	
Greeting cards	Make and sell your own cards		Card, colored pencils, photos	Sales permit	Sell your handmade cards in sets	
Inventions						
Model plane maker	Making and fixing model aircraft		Glue, paint	None	Advertise at school to save kids from having to fix models they don't have time to fix	

Selling services (side label)

Selling services (side label)

Selling

techniques

Once you've decided what you're going to sell and come to grips with the money and equipment you may need to get started—you're ready to go. Now you need customers, people who will buy what you have to offer. Without them you won't even get off the ground. And your customers may be specific to your business, so if you're doing something even a little unusual, you'll have to build your customer list from scratch.

You don't want to waste time trying to sell your product or service to someone who clearly would never want it—selling meat casseroles to vegetarians, and so on. It pays to do a little research and figure out where your target market is likely to be found. This research will help you set your prices and help you decide where and when to advertise.

You've probably been persuading people to do things for you most of your life—"Mom, can you get me a pizza for supper tonight?" "Dad, can you drive me to the football game tomorrow, please?" You've probably gotten your own way more times than not.

You'll need the same techniques when selling products:

- Set your goals—know what you want to do for your customers and what you want from them.

- Use a friendly voice. Say please and thank you. Smile. Look as if you're expecting a yes—after all you're young, and people usually like helping young people.

- If you get an iffy no, don't give up. Smile again and offer a little more information. Is there anything they didn't understand? Leave your flier or business card. Tell them about other happy customers and say you hope you can come back another time.

- If you get a firm negative, leave your flier or business card. Say you hope you'll be able to help in the future—and move on. Approach the next person.

- Don't dwell on a no—there's a yes just around the corner.

You only get about 3% of actual sales from cold calling, but you are getting your name out there. And next time, who knows!

The paperwork

Sadly, there's one part of running a business that's a lot like being in school—and that's the paperwork. All kinds of information must be recorded, either on paper or on your computer. It's worth setting up the books before you get going and while you're not too busy. Look back at your business plan, and remember all the things you said you would need to do. Then invest in some files and notebooks and start to fill them in on a regular basis.

Your letterhead

You can print your letterhead onto blank sheets when you need them. The same goes for invoices to customers.

Your company registration

If you're setting yourself up as a one-man band or sole trader, and don't plan on making loads of cash overnight, you don't need to record your details with anyone at this point. However, later, you might want to register your activity with the proper authorities.

Your schedule

Keep an accurate diary of everything that happens in your business. Don't let a bad memory damage it.

Your accounts

Keep a receipt for every single purchase, however small. You'll be amazed at how these add up and help reduce your tax payments at the end of the year. If you throw away the receipts, you'll be paying tax twice! The clearer and more accurate your accounts, the easier it will be to assess whether your business is succeeding wildly or failing wildly—or steadily ticking along. Without records, you'll be banking on guesswork, and that's a sure way to disaster.

Mansumandig
(Taking Risks)

In a small village in the Philippines lived a man and his wife.

So the man took the 25 centavos, bought half a bag of rice, and carried it on his shoulders to the miners. They bought the rice for 25 centavos, and the man was glad, because his shoulder had started to ache. Asked if they wanted more, the miners said yes …

The next day the man sold his rice as before, and did the same thing for the rest of the year.

With the hemp she made varos, which she sold for 12 centavos per varo. She did this all year.

When she next did the accounts, she sat her husband opposite her again. After taking away the 25 centavos, she had 300 pesos left. Her husband leaned against the wall and thought.

But rather than being angry or self-satisfied, she gave him money to buy a water buffalo, which he used to plow the fields. They were well-off from then on.

At the year's end, his wife did the accounts. When she heard how her husband had been selling the rice for the same price he'd bought it at, she was shocked. He only had the same 25 centavos he started with a year before!

His wife asked him to give her the money, and she went to the fields and purchased 25 centavos worth of hemp.

Dead rich!

Today when we think of the famous, we usually throw in "rich" as well, because famous people, we think, are bound to be rich. Look at all those pop stars on TV that show you around their million-dollar homes and fleets of cars. These people have money. Then there are the sports stars. Some of them earn more in a week than most people do in a year. Both the pop stars and sports stars will say that they deserve what they get because they have talent, and talent should be rewarded. We all believe talent should be rewarded. What we don't expect is that talented people will end up dying poor and being buried in a pauper's grave. Some very famous people didn't enjoy the rewards their talent and work deserved.

No sale

On May 15, 1990, a painting called *Portrait of Dr. Gachet* sold at Christies in New York for $82.5 million. On November 19, 1998, a painting called *Self-Portrait Without Beard* by the same artist sold for $71.5 million. Sales like that should have made the artist a multimillionaire. But they didn't. In fact, during his own lifetime this artist sold just one painting, **The Red Vineyard**. His name was Vincent van Gogh, and despite his great talent, he died a poor man.

Van Gogh was born in Holland in 1853. He was the son of a pastor and was brought up in a religious and cultured household. He first worked as a clerk in a bookstore, an art salesman, and even a preacher, although he was fired for being a bit too enthusiastic! What he really wanted to be, though, was an artist. He said he wanted to give happiness to others by creating beauty. He obviously didn't do it for the money.

So Van Gogh studied art and experimented with a style known as impressionism, with an emphasis on light and color. Today his works are worth millions. But his lack of business sense and the fact that his paintings were ahead of the times, meant he was penniless. Extremely depressed and suffering from mental illness, he shot himself to death in 1890.

Pop star composer

When Leopold Mozart, a Salzburg, Austria, royal chamber musician, recognized that his young son Wolfgang was a little special, he decided to set out on a tour across Europe. Wolfgang was just 6 years old, but he could play the piano and he enthralled audiences. By the age of 8 he had written three symphonies.

Wolfgang Amadeus Mozart went on to become a famous composer and pianist, and millions admire his work even today. He is one of the best-loved composers ever. During his own lifetime he was almost the equivalent of a modern pop star, playing to enthusiastic audiences and composing music for royalty. But, like van Gogh, he died poor, with barely enough money in his pocket to pay for a pauper's burial.

When Mozart lived and worked, composers were paid for writing a piece of music, for physically playing it, or for conducting. There were no performance rights or copyright laws, just one sum of money paid for one performance. So although he was clearly a genius, Mozart had to make extra money by giving piano and composition lessons. He did get a regular income for a while as the royal court composer for the emperor.

It was difficult to make ends meet, though, because he was mixing in very affluent society and needed to spend a lot just to keep up. Later, when he became less popular, he simply had no way of earning a lot of money. Although things were beginning to improve a little at the time, he died at age 35, in debt with just a little money in his pocket.

Lord of the rights

If we had to think of a series of books as popular as the Harry Potter adventures by J.K. Rowling, we'd probably think of *The Hobbit* and The Lord of the Rings trilogy by J.R.R. Tolkien. Both series have been made into movies, and J.K..Rowling has made even more millions from the sale of the movie rights. You'd probably think, then, that Tolkien would have done the same. But Tolkien did not die a rich man.

The popularity of *The Hobbit*, which was published in 1937, prompted Tolkien's publisher to ask for a sequel. It took Tolkien 12 years to write *The Lord of the Rings*. The trilogy had a huge following by the time of Tolkien's death in 1973, and the books were just beginning to earn quite a bit of money.

The real money was yet to come, however. The film rights to Tolkien's stories had been bought by a man called Saul Zaentz, an American film producer. So when Peter Jackson made his series of films based on the books, it wasn't Tolkien or even his family who reaped the rewards, it was Zaentz. After lawsuits and lots of arguments, Zaentz made nearly $200 million from a work of art he had nothing to do with creating!

Copyright

If there is a moral to be learned from these stories it's that talent isn't always recognized when talented people are alive. And even if it is, the rewards may take years to come—years when you are old and need money, or even after your death. The rewards may even go to someone else!

Today everyone knows the value of talent and creation. Artists, musicians, and authors protect the value of their creations under an international law called copyright. This is the right of everyone who creates a work to own that right and the benefits that come from it. If they die, they can pass those rights on to whomever they like.

Many countries have signed on to the copyright laws, so if the work is published or broadcast abroad—even on the Internet—the user must respect the laws.

Royalties

So, if you create a work of talent that is published or recorded or used in some way for many people to enjoy, you will automatically own the copyright in it. And by owning the copyright, you also benefit from any money that comes from its use or sale. Whenever a copy of your work is made or recorded, you will earn a part of the profit from that sale. This part of the profit is known as a royalty.

Today, people who rely on their talent to earn money have loads of advisers and managers to help them deal with the money they earn. There are also special agencies all over the world that monitor and collect royalties and register the works properly. After all, these rewards could keep them wealthy for the rest of their lives.

Sharing your money

It's all too easy to grow up in your own world and close your eyes to what's going on outside. But every headline on TV or in the newspaper is trying to inform you about problems and injustices outside the comfort of your home. Do you care about what goes on in the world and the people who share it with you? If you plan to do something useful with your life, to be a citizen of the planet—and not a passive potato—then there's no time like the present for starting to take an interest.

Fund-raising

There's a charity walk planned. You have to walk around your local park and some outlying woods in a sponsored event. For each mile that you walk, various friends and family will sponsor you to the tune of 50 cents a mile. If you complete the walk, you'll raise $5 per sponsor. You could walk as a group, as a whole family, or your class at school could get involved. Suddenly you're raising $150. And if there are another 50 people doing the same as you, that's big bucks!

Giving to others

There are many, many people on our planet who need help. If you watch television news reports, or even see appeals in newspapers, you must be aware of how difficult life is for people in poor countries or war-torn places or areas devastated by hurricanes. We all have needs and wants. Needs are things that we can't do without—things like food, water, and clothing. Wants are things that we THINK we can't do without—things like ice cream, video games, and designer clothes. But of course we can do without some of these "wants" so we can help others.

When you see pictures of refugees and the horror they're living through, it's difficult to see what you can do to help. But the saying "Every little bit helps" really does work here.

Giving to others less well-off than yourself is not about going around feeling pious and smug. It's about knowing that someone out there will eat today because of what you've done. And that has to make you feel you've done something worthwhile.

How much?

How much you give is entirely up to you, of course. Settle on an amount you feel comfortable with, and remember that however small this is, by giving regularly, the donation starts to build into something really meaningful. And don't forget that giving money is just one way of helping. You can give toys, books, and clothes—it all helps.

Tax

If you earn money and pay income tax, you can deduct the value of money or gifts that you give to charity from your taxable income. The government does this to encourage people to give to charity, so make sure you keep a record of everything you donate.

Charities

Charities are organizations that give help in many different forms to those in need. There are many well-known charities you will have heard of—and maybe helped from time to time. These have an excellent reputation for rushing to a disaster zone and bringing immediate relief. They also work over the long term, to improve education and health wherever they are based.

Foundations are also charities. These are set up by wealthy companies, individuals, or families to support certain projects with cash. Community foundations can be established to use specific funds for charitable purposes. They don't pay taxes, so they get the full benefit of their (and your) money.

Philanthropists

Philanthropists are defined as people who feel goodwill toward their fellow citizens, people who make the effort to promote human welfare. This definition doesn't mention money, but today, philanthropists almost always donate money to good works. Bill Gates, chairman of Microsoft and currently the richest man in the world, is said to be worth $51 billion. He and his wife have formed the Bill and Melinda Gates Foundation and have given it billions of dollars to spend on health and learning projects around the world.

Sponsorship

There are lots of opportunities to help children by sponsoring individuals or contributing to projects run through their communities or schools. Under these projects, you donate a small amount each month, which is taken automatically from your bank account and transferred to the charity and cause of your choice. This kind of giving is easy to organize in school, particularly if you're helping to establish or equip a school like your own in a severely deprived area at home or abroad.

Lives are changed forever

Of course, the lives of sponsored children are changed for the better as a result of your financial gifts. The children benefit from much-needed education and can attend and thrive at school, get basic medical care, and hygiene education. The families benefit as well, through programs that provide training for parents so that they can better support themselves.

But the children also benefit in ways you can't even imagine. What you provide through a simple letter may be the encouragement a struggling girl or boy needs to make it through another day.

Rubina's Story of Success

Rubina was a sponsored child in Save the Children's sponsorship program beginning in 1981 in Bangladesh. At 7 years of age, she received her first letter from her sponsor, who was waiting anxiously to hear back from her. It was exciting to learn that she had a foreign friend interested in her and her future. In Bangladesh, girls typically have less access to education and as a result, fewer life choices. However, because of her sponsor, she was able to participate in academic, cultural, and physical fitness activities. Over the years, she won many awards and finally graduated from high school and college. She became a teacher, working for one of Save the Children's partners.

You and your money

You've read lots about money in this book, about how you get to money and how money gets to you. You've also found out that what happens after that is entirely up to you. You're already thinking about what you can do with the money in your pocket, what you can do to get more, and what the future holds.

Even if you felt at the start of the book that you were a bit young to start managing your money, you now know that you're not! You are already a CONSUMER, an earner, a spender, and a saver. You've read how exciting and challenging it can be to work for yourself and for others, what huge opportunities for young people are out there—and how much help you can get if you look for it.

So now it's time to think about yourself and how you fit into this global world of money.

Put a few new labels on yourself

- The role of young people in the economy is growing and this involves YOU.
- You're not just a consumer; you're already an important part of the economy.
- Young people have never had so much money, and spending isn't the only thing you can do with it! It's time to get started on money management.
- Jobs for younger people are set to change. There will be more positions, more openings to go it alone, and more power and responsibility to do so.
- You're young. You may be inexperienced but you have assets to sell—you can be polite, punctual, bright, responsible, and honest. People will invest in you for these reasons. And none of these will cost you anything.

The future is all before you. You are probably more money-wise than your parents were at your age—and the opportunities before you are also far greater.

The feel-good factor

There's no doubt that money is an important factor in how you feel. It's at the root of much of what you want to do and what you can and can't do. By managing your money successfully, you'll be able to avoid all the problems of debt and the worry that goes with it. Putting a little aside, spending wisely, making contributions to a charity or helping others less well off, setting goals, engaging in work, using your skills, and meeting challenges—will all build your feel-good factor.

Unfortunately there are still many young adults who think they can buy happiness—that they can communicate who they are in society through the purchases they make. They jump from this possession to that, thinking it's going to buy them some sort of inner peace. But it's an artificial high. In the end, it leaves them feeling hollow.

Being a young person in today's society isn't easy. Lots of people expect something from you. Some days everything goes right; on other days nothing does. Many people will say that it's the bad times that teach you the most. So learning to enjoy all of the good things in life is as important as learning to cope with the bad things.

Feeling good!

Can money make you happy?

Many people think that if they were richer they'd be happier. Of course, people who have enough to be able to feed and clothe themselves and live a comfortable life are far happier than those who don't. But once you are comfortable, does having more money bring more happiness? Well, being rich doesn't guarantee happiness, and being rich isn't the ONLY way to be happy.

People who think wealth and happiness go together can find themselves on an upward slope—always struggling to be richer and richer, and becoming more and more unhappy because they can't make it. In the end, they feel as if they've failed—they never quite made it to the top. However, feeling content

with what you've achieved is probably the key to happiness. Indeed, someone with fewer needs and far fewer wants is set to be happier than someone who's always looking for more.

What the surveys say

Do money and happiness go hand in hand? Market surveys often produce different results. Some state quite clearly that people who have less money are not as happy as those who have more. Others show equally clearly that you can be happy or miserable no matter how much you have in the bank—being happy is about counting your blessings, whatever your earning power.

Most surveys agree on these points:

- Once you have enough to be comfortable, your state of happiness doesn't grow by leaps and bounds as you get richer.
- Sometimes the more you have, the more insecure and worried you become that you might lose it all.
- Some people take well-paid jobs they hate, just because they pay a high salary. This means they spend one-third of their lives, from Monday to Friday, feeling miserable!

Money ethics

Ethics are a code of conduct that helps determine what is good, right, and proper. They are moral principles. But can making money and ethics go hand in hand?

You've heard it said that money is the root of all evil, right? Wrong! This is said to be a quote from the Bible, but what the prophet Paul actually said was, "For the love of money is the root of all kinds of evil." A clear distinction must be made between the LOVE of money and money itself.

But the majority of people in the world aren't rich at all—they're incredibly poor. Mother Teresa was certainly a blessed woman and she had no wealth at all—she chose to live among the poor without the distraction of possessions. And there are many others who teach that fulfillment is not to be found in "keeping up with the Joneses."

The bottom line is that money, like technology, is neutral. It can be used for good, or evil. Most religions deal with the motives behind moneymaking and the use of money. If the motives are pure, then what money buys can be very good. And of course, the true measure of wealth is to love people, and not the things that money can buy.

Glossary

accounts
Accounts are statements that record the profit earned by a business and the money owed to that business.

asset
An asset is an item of value owned by a person or a business.

balance
The balance is an amount of money owed. It is also the amount remaining when the items in an account have been added up.

bank account
Each customer of a bank has a bank account that records the movement of their money in and out.

banknote
A banknote is a piece of paper, issued by a government, that is used as money.

blacklist
To blacklist means to bar someone from receiving something because you no longer trust them.

bond
A bond is a printed piece of paper which records a loan of money made to a government.

bonus
A bonus is extra money paid out to a person as a reward.

bottom line
Bottom line is the business term used to describe the net profits or losses of a company.

bronze
Bronze is a metal made of copper and tin, once used to make coins.

budget
A budget is an estimate of money expected to be paid or received sometime in the future.

burglary
A burglary is a theft of possessions from a building.

business plan
A business plan is a document that sets out the future activities and goals of a company.

charity
A charity is an organization set up to help those people who cannot afford, or who cannot get, the help they need.

check
A check is a printed piece of paper that orders a bank to pay money out of a customer's account.

cost of living
The cost of living is a standard used to describe the cost to a family of buying essential goods and services.

counterfeit
Counterfeit describes something that is a forgery or a fake.

cowrie shell
Cowrie shells are seashells that were once used like coins to barter or exchange goods.

credit
Credit is an arrangement a customer can make to pay for goods at a later date.

credit card
A credit card is a plastic card used to buy goods and services to be paid for at a later date.

credit rating
Your credit rating is a score held by banks or credit agencies that decides how much debt you might be able to borrow, based on your past record of earnings, loans, and repayments.

creditor
A creditor is anyone who provides goods or services and who does not collect their money after they have delivered.

debtor's prison
In the past, a person in debt could be imprisoned in a debtor's prison until the debts were repaid.

deposit
A deposit is an amount of money paid in advance for goods that have not yet been bought or delivered.

discount
A discount is a reduced price.

earnings
Earnings are the amount of money paid to someone for doing a job.

economy
The economy of a country is everything to do with the way it produces things and sells them.

electronic transfer
An electronic transfer describes the way money is passed from one account to another by computer.

entrepreneur

An entrepreneur is a businessperson who organizes, manages, and assumes the risks of a business.

environmentally friendly

Products and services that do not damage the planet are said to be environmentally friendly.

ethics

Ethics are a code of behavior that sets out how people should behave in a fair and proper manner.

expenditure

Expenditure is money that has been spent.

finance company

A finance company provides money to people and companies that wish to borrow money.

forecast

A forecast is an estimate of how much a person or company will earn in a year.

foundation

A foundation is an organization set up to carry out charitable activities.

gamble

To gamble means to take a risk to make money.

grant

A grant is another name for an allowance that is given to a person or company by the government or by some other organization.

gross

Gross means complete earnings with no tax deducted.

Inca

The Inca were an Indian civilization that once lived in the Andes Mountains of South America.

inheritance

An inheritance is an amount of money or goods received as a gift on someone's death.

interest

Interest is the price a lender charges to someone who is borrowing money. It is a percentage of the value of the loan.

invest

To invest means to spend money in order to earn more money.

invoice

An invoice is a list of costs charged for work done or supplies made.

lend

To lend means to allow someone to borrow your money or goods.

limited company (Ltd.)

A limited company is a company whose shareholders have no responsibility for its debts if their shares are paid for.

lottery

A lottery is a way of raising money by selling numbered tickets.

matrilineal inheritance

Matrilineal inheritance describes a system where the females, not the males, in a family inherit the family goods and money.

minimum wage

The minimum wage is the least money that can be paid by law to a worker for doing a job.

moneylender

A moneylender is someone who lends money and charges interest to the borrower.

net

Net describes the value of something after any necessary deductions have been made.

net worth

A person's net worth is the value of their wealth estimated by banks and other financial organizations.

niche market

A niche market describes the group of customers who will buy a special product or service that no other business is selling.

note

A note is a shortened word for a banknote, or any form of paper money.

overdraft

An overdraft is a form of loan made by a bank to a customer.

patrilineal inheritance

Patrilineal inheritance describes a system where the males, not the females, in a family inherit the family goods and money.

pension

A pension is a regular allowance paid to people over a certain age.

philanthropist

A philanthropist is a rich person who gives large sums of money to good and charitable causes.

pocket money
Pocket money is a regular allowance given to young people by their parents or caregivers.

primogeniture
Primogeniture describes the system of inheritance where the eldest child inherits all family goods and money.

profit
Profit is the money earned when income is greater than expenditure.

red packet
A red packet is a small money gift handed out in China on special occasions.

resume
A resume is a report on your work skills and experience.

revenue
Revenue is the money that a company or person receives.

savings account
A savings account records the money saved by someone in a bank.

savings bond
A savings bond is a form of investment that earns interest.

self-employment
To be self-employed means to work for yourself.

share
A share is a part of the capital, or wealth, of a company. Shares are sold by a company to raise money.

smelt
To smelt means to melt down a metal and remove any impurities in it.

spending power
Spending power describes the wealth of a section of the population.

sponsor
To sponsor means to support someone by giving them money on a regular basis.

stock
A stock is a form of investment, usually money lent to the government.

target market
A target market is the group of people selected by a company to advertise and sell goods.

tax
Tax is the money paid by people and companies to the government to help fund the running of the country.

tool coin
A tool coin was a coin made in the shape of a working tool, used to buy and sell goods in the past.

trust fund
A trust fund is an amount of money, valuables or property set aside for someone's benefit.

unit of value
A unit of value is something that everyone agrees has a set worth.

USP (unique selling point)
A USP describes the special quality in a product or service that will attract the customer away from the competition.

Want to Learn More?

At the Library

Berg, Adriane G., and Arthur Berg Bochner. *The Totally Awesome Money Book for Kids*, 2nd edition. New York: Newmarket Press, 2002.

Harman, Hollis Page. *Money Sense for Kids!* 2nd ed. Hauppauge, N.Y.: Barron's, 2004.

Nathan, Amy. *The Kids' Allowance Book*. New York: Walker and Company, 1998.

Kiefer, Jeanne. *Jobs for Kids: A Smart Kid's Q&A Guide*. Brookfield, Conn.: Millbrook Press, 2003.

Look for all the books in this series:

Common Cents
The Money in Your Pocket
0-7565-1671-4

Cowries, Coins, Credit
The History of Money
0-7565-1676-5

Get Rich Quick?
Earning Money
0-7565-1674-9

Money: It's Our Job
Money Careers
0-7565-1675-7

Save, Spend, Share
Using Your Money
0-7565-1672-2

What's It All Worth?
The Value of Money
0-7565-1673-0

On the Web

For more information on *the money in your pocket*, use FactHound to track down Web sites related to this book.

1. Go to *www.facthound.com*
2. Type in a search word related to this book or this book ID: 0756516714
3. Click on the *Fetch It* button.
   FactHound will fetch the best Web sites for you!

Index

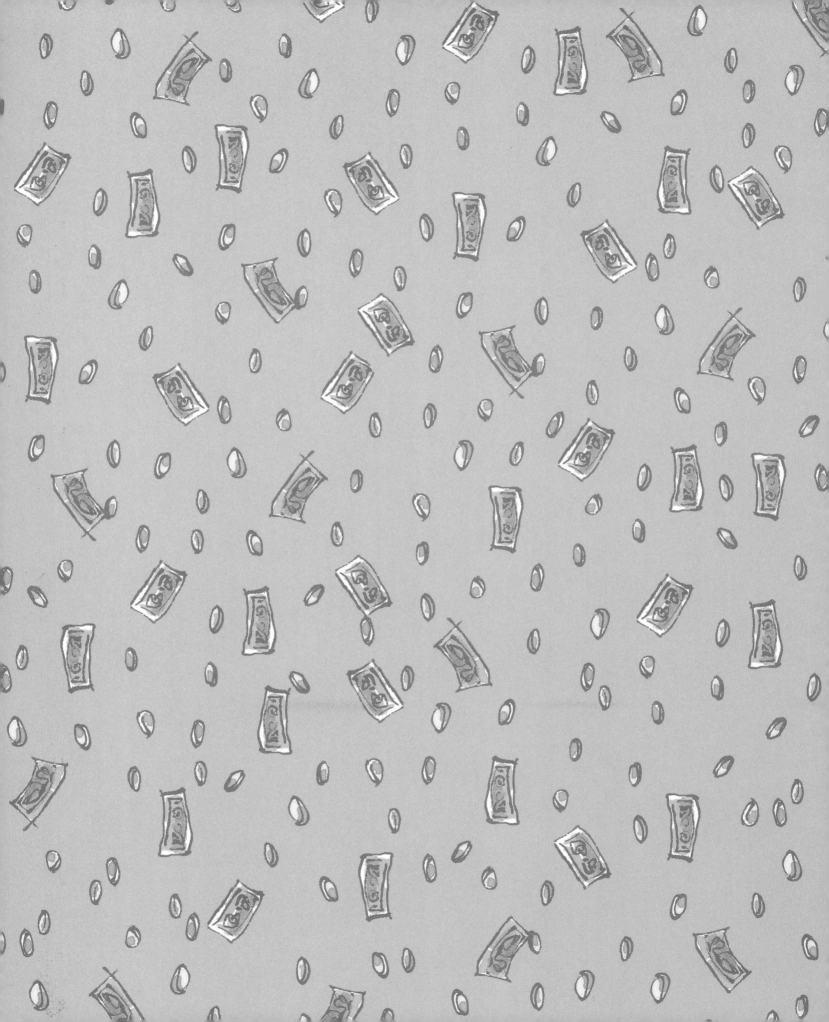